I0758196

PEACEFUL MIND

FOR A

BLISSFUL LIFE

Master Your Beliefs, Meditate To Conquer Stress, And Learn 6 Mindfulness Secrets To Build A Better Life

JOSEPH NEYYAN
(neyyanjoseph@gmail.com)

Table of Content

materials. Any perceived slight of any individual or organization is purely unintentional.

ABOUT AUTHOR

Exploring the world of books, researching writers, read author blogs, and more. Attended the 'CMS Higher Secondary School' which is affiliated to Central Board of Secondary Education, New Delhi. After completing the formal part of his education, he graduated from the Indira Gandhi National Open University, New Delhi, thereafter enrolled in the Army and served the nation for 28 long years and retired as a Junior Commissioned Officer.

Now enjoying the privilege of being able to write full time, he is committed to producing books on nonfiction (personal development) that not only inspire and challenge people but also inspire in living life that is more rewarding and fulfilling. He is also a blogger, You Tuber, Wellness Coach and Author of three books in series.

ACKNOWLEDGEMENT

First of all, I thank the Almighty for making this book possible. I wish to thank my Mom, Mrs. Mary George and Dad Late Mr. NT George, who gave birth to me in this earth and made capable to lead the journey of writing this book. My wife Mrs. Litty Joseph, who not only recognized in me that flair for writing my thoughts but also gave me the opportunity to write in my 'her time'.

I don't want to miss out on all the friends, mentor who are pursuing Masters with me, mentioning about both the departments, yet all your encouragement on this news added new feathers on my cap. To my entire family and wonderful people who have imbibed positivity in me and those I couldn't take names of, I cannot thank you enough.

And lastly, to all the readers who chose to give my book a read and gather all the courage in analyzing the honest positive views.

INTRODUCTION

"The greatest discovery of my generation is that human beings can alter their lives by altering their attitudes of mind, "–William James.

There was a crow, took a piece of flesh from the Butcher shop and flew up happily. Suddenly a group of eagles' followed the crow to attack. The crow flew fast but unable to fly as the eagles were so speed than the crow. In the meantime a Garud (large Eagle bird) met the crow while flying in the sky and asked the reason about the tension of flying so speed. The crow said that the eagles are chasing it from the beginning and it fearing of its life's danger.

The Garud said the reason the eagles are chasing because of the piece of flesh in the mouth. So Garud asked the crow to leave the piece of flesh and you will be safe from the eagles and there no danger for its life and live happily. The Crow opened its mouth and the piece of flesh fall down to the earth. The eagles were going back to the flesh to catch and the Crow become safe. We human being are holding the piece of flesh in our mouth and create unhappy for the entire life.

Here flesh I mean is Angry, Ego, Comparative, Arrogant, and Jealousy, which we hold at every time and unable to separate from our life. So we face unhappy always in our life. We have to change our habit in order to put an end to Angry, Ego, Comparative, Arrogant, and Jealousy and have a peaceful mind for a blissful life. We may lift whatever challenges or difficulty faced to the God and live happily till the end of our life. This life is only once we get an opportunity on the earth to live and make it peacefully and blissfully.

The time of birth and death are with God's hand, but the time in between the life is within our hand. So live your life peacefully and blissfully, and the world should say after our dead 'Wow!!! What a life he had lived'.

Where there is love, there's no place for force, and where there is force, there's no place for love. It's like saying where there is darkness, there cannot be light and vice versa–(1 John 4:8,16).

Happiness is coming from own as it is not sell in any shop or mall. Everyone wanted to be happy in this world but don't know the process to lead the goal. Happiness, therefore, is an expression of our inner joy, not a product what we make. The desire for happiness and the desire for meaning are deeply interlinked, and that is why we cannot achieve happiness without purpose. People think that if they get the desired things, then they become happy. If they not get, then they are disappointed.

Expectation is the enemy of the happiness. People expect many more things like parents wanted their children to study well and well disciplined, Student expect to get more marks from all the examination and businessman expect more profits like goes on.

Happiness is like waves in the seashore. It comes and goes and vice versa. Some of them think that money makes them happy, but the statement is wrong. Viktor Frankl once astutely observed that "Happiness cannot be pursued, it must ensue". Happiness and sadness are the 2 inseparable sides of a coin. Osho correctly said that money and every day meditation brings peace, happy and joyful life.

My ultimate reason for writing this book is to help people understand the importance of using their life to the fullest by living in a peaceful mind for a blissful life. And if this book can do that for even one person, it fulfil my purpose for writing this book. Hope you may be the right person.

Chapter 1: What is bliss?

One reason this is so difficult is because some words used to describe it are also difficult to define. Bliss is where happiness, meaning, and truth coverage. Bliss is found in every religion but does not require a specific religion in order to know it. Bliss is the ultimate state of consciousness that every religion holds as its highest goal and achievement, though each uses different terminology to explain it. Whether we are Christian or Hindu, Jewish or Muslim, Buddhist or atheist, Wiccan or animist, Taoist or Native American, we all strive for bliss.

The Secrets to Finding Bliss

How come more of us don't know about or haven't experienced bliss? First, we should note it that many of us do sometimes have glimpses of bliss, but as quickly as those glimpses come, they vanish. We usually don't fully understand what we've experienced or how to reproduce it- or even whether it can be reproduced. The root problem is that we are looking in the wrong places. Happiness, meaning, and truth can never come from externalities such as luxury goods, celebrity, social engineering, psychoanalysis, political systems, or even through professing superficial belief in religious dogmas. We look for them everywhere except the one place they truly live: inside ourselves.

The secret to finding bliss is simple: it is reversing our orientation inwardly instead of outwardly, of removing and revealing. We must strip away our expectations and learned beliefs that external conditions can truly satisfy us. Instead, we must learn to identify, appreciate, and tap into the reservoir of super satisfaction that is already extant inside us, requiring no external environment, situation, or circumstance.

What does bliss mean: Dictionary definitions?

Let's start with three dictionary definitions of bliss as under:
1. Cambridge - Perfect happiness.
2. Oxford - Perfect happiness; great joy.
3.Merriam-Webster: Perfect happiness, paradise, heaven.

So bliss is the same as happiness, is it? Well, not really, because most people would agree that perfect happiness is not the same at all as just happiness. According to the dictionary, be perfectly happy to be blissful. So feeling blissful means feeling perfectly happy.

How To Live A Peace And Blissful Mind

A lot of individuals have the misconception that riches and wealth are the only tangible resources able to usher in happiness into our lives. This is wrong and, to a large extent, untrue. Although money plays a big part in keeping your mind off problems, there are several other things that can make you feel good. When you recognize the things that frequently get you excited, you can concentrate on doing these activities more, and set these activities high in your to-do list.

True happiness comes from the heart because that's where most of our feelings, both positive and negative, come from. To live a life full of happiness, you must substitute the negative feelings in your mind for positive ones. This would essentially make you look forward to a new day, bustling with events that secure your happiness and allow your experience new adventures, positively shocking and funny happenings, and a few low points, which can't be avoided. If you want to turn your life around into experiencing several happy and blissful days, you need to understand that both shades of feelings, positive and negative, need to be controlled. Here are a few other tips you can follow to live a blissful life.

Mind the words that come out of your mouth

Once you utter words from your mouth, they can never be taken back. A mind that intermittent processes words to be said is highly likely to say all the right stuff. A lot of individuals that live blissful, happy lives understand the importance of holding their tongues in situations they feel talking might escalate into an already built-up tension. Steer clear of horrible negative words like hateful words and never use on the people both in their presence or absence.

Even if you meet with a nasty person, instead of using words like 'not very pleasant'. This type of lifestyle would allow you to endear you to people in your neighborhood. This works as plus if you're a naturally kind-hearted person. Just take care of your tongue in the same way you take care of gold and silver. Your mouth should be a sugar factory. Words to come out in a sweet and polite manner.

<u>Let go of your past</u>. Your experiences in the past are tools that can help you propel yourself into the future. Smart people are highly likely to move on after their experiences since they realize it can never be wiped off and will always be an irreversible part of the present. The ability to accept your past, learn your lessons and move on, would go a long way to determining how you take control of your present situations.

To move on from traumatic experiences, such as an abusive spouse or partner, take precautions to cut them off from your life not only physically, but digitally. This will ensure that your new life is clear of prompts that will induce further emotional turmoil.

You can also find other friends or relatives going through or about to go through the same experience you've had in the past and help them with their trying periods. Your past will play a big role in either building up or diminishing your self-esteem. Harnessing your experiences to enhance your self-esteem would go a long way in helping you lead a peace, blissful life.

<u>Love your body</u>. The focus on the body shape and size has been increased in recent times. Everyone wants to keep their bodies toned to look acceptable by other people. Maintaining your body requires you to pay close attention to what your body needs and satisfy it with nutritious foods that provide you with energy and improve your mood. Your body is a big part of being happy through the day, and it needs to be filled with many vitamins.

To keep your body and health in great shape, you must engage in games and sports to help you look younger. Also, you need to balance your mental needs alongside your physical needs. The state of your mind basically determines your physical appearance.

Mind your Business. Many people like to spend large amounts of time talking about the lives of others. They also love to degrade the subjects of their discussion and make judgments about every action the subject takes, criticize the subject's lifestyle, and gossip about the subject. This kind of despicable activity ensures one focuses energy on another person's life.

If you can take your time to analyze your life and solve the problems bothering you instead of dwelling on the actions of other people, you could live a blissful life. Minding your business would give you the ability to live freely without issues from other people and allow you to relish in life's adventures.

Be close to positive people. There's proverb that goes, 'show me your friend and I'll tell you who you are'. This gives credence to the fact that your circle of friends largely determines how you think and the way you see the world. Friends mostly have common goals and ambitions. That's particularly why you need to surround yourself with positive, optimistic people. Being around those that think negatively about every situation would have an adverse impact on your life.

Each person has something they're great at. If your circle of friends always tries to put down your ideas and ambitions and mentally weigh you down from reaching your potential, you need to cut them off. What can help propel you to greater heights are friends who see the good in your ideas, and positively critique them? Friends like these would help you spread your wings and glide along in the journey that's called life.

Be Generous. Many people are usually greedy and even though they have a lot, find it hard to give to those who need. You need to be generous with either your money, time, energy or passion with individuals. Feeling like you're doing good for people helps to make you happy and fulfilled. In fact, some people make it their life's ambition to see others happy. Giving money to charities and spending time with people to listen to their problems are actions covered under the umbrella of generosity.

You improve your life, be happy, and cut off things that make you sad and depressed. You need to keep in mind that those who never give up will eventually get to achieve their goals. The steps to living a peaceful, blissful life, start with breaking the ice on actions like being generous, minding your business, and letting go of your past.

Chapter 2: How To Happy: 9 Ways To Find More Bliss In Life

The famous pursuit is so powerful that it has its own holiday, with March 20 set aside by the United Nations to recognize contentment as a universal goal for people everywhere.

"After much consideration, I believe that the purpose of life is to find happiness," The Dalai Lama written in *"The Book of Joy,"* his volume with Archbishop Desmond Tutu.

"From the very core of our being, we simply desire joy and contentment. But so often, these feelings are fleeting and hard to find".

An entire industry wants to teach you how to make those feelings last. There are classes and even the *Journal of Happiness* studies to put an academic spin on the findings.

But all this intense pressure to be happy has spawned a backlash, with books such as *"America the Anxious: How Our Pursuit of Happiness Is Creating a Nation of Nervous Wrecks"* now competing for your attention.

Remember, you do really have some power to reach bliss: Genes determine 50 percent of your happiness, while circumstances account for 10 percent. That leaves 40 percent up to you, studies have shown. Here are nine tips to get you started:

1. **<u>Focus on relationships</u>**. If you had to name one key to happiness, it would be relationships, said Gretchen Rubin, author of *"The Happiness Project"*. That means romantic relationships, friendships, close ties with siblings and colleagues- any meaningful and deep bonds with people you like.

If you're thinking about how to be happier, thinking about how to deepen or broaden your relationships is probably a great place to start, Rubin said. "We need to have enduring, intimate relationships. We need to confide. We need to feel like we belong".

2. **<u>Don't fall for the trap of thinking, "I will be happy when......"</u>**. You may think you'll finally find bliss when you get married or get a promotion or win the lottery. But events you think will make you happy often don't.

"People think it's going to be perfect as soon as this 'thing' happens, but no. It has a very short-term effect," said Catherine Sanderson, a psychology professor at Amherst College. "One challenge is that we just adapt to it".

3. **<u>Don't look to money for happiness</u>**. Once you make \$75,000 a year, money doesn't have much of an effect on your contentment, one study found. Here's what the Dalai Lama said in *"The Book of Joy"*:

"The ultimate source of happiness is within us. Not money, not power, not status. Some of my friends are billionaires, but they are very unhappy people. Power and money cannot bring inner peace. Outward attainment will not bring real inner joyfulness. We must look inside".

4. **<u>Be Authentic</u>**. To add more joy to your life, know yourself. Take the Saturday morning test, recommended Neil Pasricha, director of The Institute for Global Happiness.

What do you like to do on a Saturday morning when you don't have to do anything? Cook? Play guitar? Work out? The answer reveals what your natural passions are. Boost your happiness by incorporating more of these activities into your life and work.

5. Do something nice for somebody else and talk with others. People who engage in random acts of kindness boost their well-being. That includes small gestures and bigger ones, like donating money to charity, said Yale University professor Laurie Santos, who teaches "Psychology and the

Good Life," the most popular class in the history of Yale College.

One of Santos' favorite studies found people who spent money on others reported greater happiness, with such generosity bestowing a "warm glow" on the givers.

Another favorite study discovered that a simple act of connecting with a stranger-talking to somebody on a train or a plane, for example–can boost your mood. We underestimate other people's interest in connecting, but such simple exchanges can be happy for everyone involved.

6. **Keep working**. Work is often the place where people are the unhappiest, so this is not about staying in a job you hate. But fulfilling, meaningful, challenging work is an important part of happiness because it provides structure and a sense of purpose, Pasricha said.

"We don't actually want to do nothing: we just want to do something we love," he noted.

Residents of Okinawa, Japan–one of the world's "Blue Zone" where people live extraordinarily long lives–don't have a word for retirement. Rather, they use "Ikigai"- which translates as "the reason you get out of bed in the morning". Work- including volunteering- often satisfies that for us, Pasricha said.

7. **<u>Move to a happy place</u>**. Hawali has once again topped the Gallup National Health and well-Being Index of the healthiest and happiest states in the nation. Residents there enjoy warm relationships, like what they do each day, love their surroundings and are inspired to treat their bodies right.

For the happiest cities, frequent winners include Naples, Florida: Boulder, Colorado: and Provo Utah.

8. **<u>Seek meaning in your life</u>**. What makes life truly worth living is meaning, said Emily Esfahani Smith, author of *"The Power of Meaning: Crafting a Life that Matters"*.

Meaning often comes from doing hard things—like raising children or starting a business—that can give you a deep sense of satisfaction. Look for ways to connect with people and find your purpose. Cherish moments that life you above the hustle and bustle of daily life, like going to church, a museum or a garden.

9. **<u>Take walks outside</u>**. Going into nature changes how your brain works: It reduces stress levels and boosts well-being, said David Strayer, a professor of psychology at the University of Utah. It's the philosophy behind forest therapy.

When you're enjoying nature, the parts of the brain associated with being mindful become more active. There's also the exercise component, which has positive effects on mood. "If you can get yourself to a park, place to walk, jog, just enjoy, be in nature and leave the phone behind for 30 minutes," Strayer said.

Chapter 3: Happiness Hacks For A Blissful Life

The all elusive, ambiguous term that everyone wants happiness, but no one seems to have. Despite living in the most comfortable time in human history, we're somehow more miserable than ever. In our efforts to become more productive and make more money, we've somehow lost sight of our personal happiness along the way.

Luckily, while we were busy making ourselves busy, science has made fantastic strides in documenting the importance of prioritizing happiness. Happy people are more productive, more creative, learn faster, have better memory, and are better problem solvers.

If this is the case, what should be the first thing you do when you wake up in the morning? Put yourself in a good mood!

Unfortunately, like many things in life, putting ourselves in a good mood is easier said than done.

The good news? I'm a happiness maniac who has devised a variety of systems to keep myself happy throughout the day. I hope that this list can help you live a life that is 10% happier. If I get you to have 1 more smile throughout the day. I have accomplished my mission. The following are the 10 hacks for a Blissful life:

1. **<u>Smile</u>**. How many times do you smile? Throughout the day? What percentage of your day do you spend with a smile on your face?

For most of us, this number is frighteningly low. In the hustle and bustle of life, we forget to do the simplest thing–smile!

Smiling is hands down the easiest way to have a happier day. Smiling releases dopamine and serotonin in the brain. It also signals your central nervous system telling your body to relax. It lowers cortisol.

Don't take it from me, I have the science to back it up. This phenomenon is known as the Facial Feedback Hypothesis, in which the facial expressions we wear influence how we feel. We've all heard the "fake it till you make it" story–this is one of those cases where it works. By wearing a smile on your face and pretending you are happy, it will make you happier and can't ask for an easier way to put yourself in a good mood.

2. **<u>Practice Gratitude</u>**. Many of us focus on the 10% is wrong with our lives, rather than the 90%

that is right. A simple trick to become happier? Flip the equation and spend your time thinking about the 90% that is good in your life. If you're from a developed country, have food to eat, clothes on your back, a place to live, and a job to provide you with money, you have it pretty good. Anytime you need a quick boost of happiness, think about the things you appreciate in life.

A 2003 study by Emmons and McCullough found that keeping a daily gratitude journal leads to better sleep, reductions in physical pain, a greater sense of wellbeing, and a better ability to handle change. It also found that practicing gratitude can lead to a 25% increase in happiness. Further, a 2008 study found that practicing gratitude directly activates the part of your brain responsible for sleep, eating, and stress management—and triggers the release of dopamine—the friendly chemical responsible for happiness and habit formation.

What does this practice look like for me? I like to spend 5 minutes every morning (usually in the shower) thinking about all the things I am grateful for in life. It's usually pretty simple too— "I'm grateful to be alive. I have food to eat, clothes to wear, a safe place to sleep, a loving family, and I'm healthy". This simple exercise will have a positive effect on every aspect of your life, from work to sleep to relationships and more.

Similarly, if you notice that you're in a bit of a funk and you're thinking about the 10% that's wrong in life, recognize this and immediately flip it to the 90%. Think about the things that are right in life, and your spirits will quickly change. Many of us have trained our minds to focus on the 10% wrong, but with some practice gratitude can become your default setting once again.

3. **Pause in Transitions**. Often the best moments to slow down and practice mindfulness are when you're transitioning from one activity to the next. Just sat down to your desk after a meeting? Wait a minute before you jump into your work. Become mindful of these small transitions. Each transition is an opportunity to take a quick break, check in with yourself to see how you're feeling, and correct course accordingly.

What does this look like for me? Before I move from one task to the next, I will set the timer on my phone 1 minute. I will then close my eyes and take 10-15 deep breaths. Throughout the day, I'll do this anywhere from 3 to 5 times. For 5 minutes a day I'm calmer, more level-headed, and notice when my emotions have the best of me. Check in with yourself throughout the day for a happier, more fulfilling life.

Feeling a bit stressed or off? Lie down on the floor for 5 minutes. I learned this one from the book *"How to live more and worry less"* by Dale Carnegie. Sometimes when I'm feeling overworked, tired, or not quite right. I'll lie down on the floor for five minutes. Contrary to many of my other techniques where I do deep breathing meditate, I'll simply let my mind wander, without trying to control it. If you want to though, you can try to focus on your breath or scan your body from head to toe (also very relaxing).

The simple act is enough time to take a quick rest, but not enough time to fall asleep. By the time the timer goes off, I'm refreshed and ready to go. The stiff floor will also give your muscles the ability to relax into it, unlike on a soft bed where your muscles can still hold tension. This also works wonders for back pain or shoulder stiffness.

4. **Go for a walk- aimlessly**. Go for a walk that is untimed with no specific destination or purpose in mind. No- walking to work or back home doesn't count either. Go for a walk for walking's sake. Go for a walk just to enjoy the simple act of walking.

In this study, people reported feeling happier after any type of physical activity other than sitting or lying down. The most common act?

Gentle walking. Literally moving in any way led to feelings of greater happiness.

Want to make it even better? Try to maintain a smile for the duration of your walk. Sounds easy, but it's insanely difficult. Every time your mind wanders, your smile will often wander with it. Maintaining the smile on your face is a great way to remain in the present moment and avoid being lost in thought.

5. **<u>Exercise is one of (if not the) most effective forms of making yourself happier quickly</u>**. Exercise releases neurotransmitters such as dopamine (the happy chemical), reduces the body's stress hormones adrenaline and cortisol, and stimulates the production of endorphins- chemicals in the brain that are the body's natural painkillers and mood elevators. It's essentially a cocktail of happiness for your brain.

Study after study found exercise to be more effective as an anti-depressant than Prozac or other common prescription medications. The mood enhancing effects of exercise also lasted longer than those of anti-depressants.

Now, I am not a medical professional and I don't recommend to stop taking your pills. Always consult with a doctor before considering this option. I'm here to present the evidence that exercise is likely equal to or potentially more effective than popping a pill every day. Give it some serious thought.

6. **<u>Dance</u>**. If all else fails, get up and dance! In a study by Dance Psychologist, Dr. Peter Lovatt researchers put people in a lab and played music for five minutes. Then they gave people three options:

(a) Sit and listen quietly to the music.
(b) Cycle on an exercise bike while they listened
or
(c) Get up and dance. All were given cognitive tasks to perform before and after.

Dr. Peter Lovatt says: "All those who danced displayed improved problem-solving skills afterwards. The same study also found that the mood levels of the dancers went up. It shows that dancing along to music even for five minutes can boost happiness and improve creative-thinking patterns".

I don't know about you, but for me there's nothing better than blasting some Michael Jackson and dancing around my room like a maniac for five minutes. I bust out the moves like no one is watching (and often no one is). I love acting like an idiot and letting the moves flow, and it has a wonderful effect on my mood.

Feeling too uptight to dance? The least you can do is put on some tunes that will put a smile on your face. Bob Marley, Michael Jackson, and Disney songs like Hakuna Matata always seem to do it for me. Create a "happy playlist" that works magic for you.

(a) **Don't go on social media.** The time you spend on social media can contribute to a lower quality of life and lower levels of happiness and wellbeing. A study conducted by the University of Pittsburgh found that the more time young adults use social media, the more likely they are to be depressed.

Get off the phone/computer, go outside, get some fresh air. Although you probably discovered this article on some form of social media, I fully encourage you to stop reading and go do one technique I've mentioned above instead.

(b) **Cold Showers**. If you can handle it cold showers improve circulation, release endorphins, reduce inflammation in the body, and improve memory and focus.

How does it work? Cold water constrict blood vessels, causing blood to flow from the surface of your body to your core. When this happens, you effectively bathe your brain and vital organs in fresh blood, helping to detoxify your body. Those same neurotransmitters I've mentioned over and over come back into the equation.

Cold water reduces cortisol, regulates serotonin levels, and floods your brain with a new buddy–norepinephrine–an adrenal hormone that can naturally improve the "feel good" effect.

When does this technique look like for me? I'll take a normal hot shower, and then for the last 2 minutes flip it on ice cold. Then, I'll flip it back to warm for the last 30 seconds to relax my blood vessels and send fresh blood back up to the surface. This is referred to as the "James Bond Shower".

Want to drive deep into the world of cold? Check out Wim-Hoff aka "The Iceman"–this dude has climbed to Everest base camp in shorts and no shirt. Truly badass. The man knows his science as well. His techniques are backed by mountains of evidence and research, and his results are no joke.

(c) **Meditate**. I saved this one for last, as it's often met with a lot of resistance and "I don't have time to meditate" but it works. There's so many options out there to get started with meditation, and the impact it will have on your life is immediately noticeable. Whether it's Headspace, Calm, or Tara Brach, you have too much to lose by not trying meditation.

There's so much evidence out there on the benefits of meditation it's hard to ignore. In case you were too lazy to check it out, one study by Fadel Zeidan, Ph.D found that be befits from meditation can be seen in as few as four 20-minute sessions. I also love this infographic on the body during meditation. (Troy Erstling)

Chapter 4: Meditation For Happiness

What do you think of when you think of happiness? Is it a feeling you chase after but never quite reach, or a state of mind that you're able to tap into if you have the right resources? Happiness is a state of mind- an underlying sense of contentment, fulfillment, and satisfaction in life.

Here's the good news: the feeling is already there, readily accessible, often buried beneath layers of thoughts and emotions. All it takes is tapping into it and reconnecting with a happy state of mind. By doing a happiness meditation, you can start mindfulness training to reconnect with that feeling and experience more happiness.

What is happiness meditation?

Achieving a sense of underlying contentment and satisfaction does not manifest itself as a wide-smile, explosive sort of happiness. Rather, it is a connection to something innate within us, leading us to this genuine sense of satisfaction and reconnection with our mind's happy state.

In practicing meditation for joy and happiness, we are creating the conditions necessary to experience a happy state of mind. To do so, we are nurturing four essential supports or ingredients of happiness: kindness, empathy, playfulness, and inner balance, by integrating these aspects of ourselves into our daily lives, we reconnect with a happy state of mind and step away from negative internal dialogue.

<u>Are we afraid of being happy?</u> If you've ever struggled with anxiety or depression, you might relate to a feeling of uneasiness, or even fear, surrounding happiness. This phenomenon is fairly common and can manifest itself differently for different people, according to research by Psychiatrist Paul Gilbert of Kingsway Hospital in England. This fear manifests itself under one of these three categories:

- Those who experience discomfort whenever they felt relaxed or even lazy.
- Those who fear experiencing happiness because they believe something bad will inevitably follow.
- Those who are conditioned to be worried and feel uncomfortable when they're not constantly worrying.

If you can identify with any of these, you're not alone—and you're also not hopeless. Through a process called neuroplasticity, the brain is able to develop and change. Practicing meditation for joy and happiness will help you become more comfortable with these ideas.

The happiness set point. It has long been thought that each of us has a happiness set point, or a fixed average amount of happiness that we naturally have within us based on genetics–but thanks to neuroplasticity, the set point can be altered. Through meditation, you can rewire your brain to reset its happiness set point. According to science, this is possible by thickening the major areas of the brain responsible for helping you cope with uncomfortable situations, and shrinking the amygdala–the part of your brain that is activated when you experience stress.

The benefits of meditating for happiness. Researchers have found that living in fear of happiness is correlated with anxiety and depression. By taking the time to nurture your mind and becoming more open to the idea of happiness, you are reducing your risk of becoming burdened by anxiety and depression. Leading a happier life and decreasing your attachment to outside circumstances can reduce stress and even help you get a better night's sleep.

Changing your perspective. Ready to get happier? First, take a moment to think about your practice. Picture yourself sitting on the side of the road and watching your thoughts, feelings, and external circumstances driving by. As you're watching them drive by, you might become unsettled by the movement. You might run into traffic and try to stop or chase after them—and become restless. As you approach your practice, try to shift your perspective toward these passing thoughts and circumstances.

One of the most effective ways to create a space of happiness within yourself is by focusing on the happiness of others. As you go through life thinking about happiness and as you try the happiness meditation outlined below, think about how the practice will benefit those around you. Think about how turning this practice into a habit can influence your relationships with other guiding you to become more present and begin seeing happiness as a matter of the present, not the future. In meditating for happiness, you might come across the visualization technique and techniques that cultivate compassion, such as loving-kindness.

Kindness—the quality of being generous and caring. Loving—someone who shows love to other people.

Blend those words together, and you capture the essence of a meditation rooted in compassion. Other mindfulness – based meditations will, by the very nature of the practice, cultivate a softer, more spacious, kinder mind, but this specific meditation places a deliberate emphasis on one purpose: to direct well-wishes and goodwill first to ourselves and then, as a ripple effect, to others.

Chapter 5: Gratitude Meditation

<u>What is gratitude meditation?</u> Gratitude meditation is simply the practice of reflecting on the things in our lives we're grateful for. It's about experiencing that feeling of appreciation, whether for a loving family member or friend, a beautiful sunny day, or the pleasure of a good cup of coffee. It can be for things large or small, tangible or intangible–perhaps a successful recovery from an injury or illness, or a tough life lesson you weathered, where you came out the other side stronger and more confident.

It is easy to get caught up in current events and the negativity of the news cycle, but in fact those things often have little to do with who we are and how we experience the world on a day-to-day basis. A grateful meditation is not about becoming desensitized to suffering or social injustice, it's a way of bringing us back to a place of personal reflection.

Research shows that gratitude is strongly and consistently associated with a greater sense of happiness and well-being. Science tells us that counting our blessings increases our optimism, relieves depression, improves immune function, and lowers blood pressure. It also strengthens our relationships with those around us.

If feeling appreciative for acts of kindness, glimpses of beauty, and the people and experiences that bring joy to our lives makes us happier, then why reserve it for just one day of the year, as Americans typically do with Thanksgiving? In this book, that's motivation enough to start a regular gratitude meditation practice. Who, what, and where fills you with a sense of gratitude?

Keeping a gratitude journal is one way to regularly note and cultivate increased appreciation and happiness about those people, things and experiences we're grateful for. Gratitude meditation is another way to express and cultivate this appreciation. Who, what, and where fills you with a sense of gratitude?

How to practice meditation for gratitude abundance. The beauty of a gratitude meditation practice is that you can do it anywhere, and of day. You could design your own personal morning gratitude meditation while you're brewing that perfect cup of coffee! Or give thanks for the abundance of food that's available to us while you're online at the grocery store. Sitting down for an evening gratitude meditation is an opportunity to mindfully reflect on the good parts of your day. Begin with a 10-minute gratitude meditation, or choose the 15 or 20- minute options. The idea is to become more familiar with the feeling of appreciation, rather than the intellectual idea, which can often sound clichéd.

The experience of appreciation is anything but, it's a heartwarming feeling that encourages to be more present. And the more familiar it becomes, the more time we're likely to spend experiencing it.

Benefits of gratitude meditation. If experiencing more feelings of happiness and appreciation isn't enough, here are a few more reasons to give thanks. According to Robert A. Emmons, Ph.D, renowned scholar on the science of gratitude, a deep sense of gratitude reduces anxiety and feelings of isolation because it takes us out of our cocoon of self-absorption and entitlement, and helps us connect to something larger than ourselves as individuals–whether to other people, nature, or a spiritual/higher power.

Another benefit, from even a short gratitude meditation, is that it can help us get unstuck. Because our brains can sometimes get caught in a loop of anxiety, worry and fear, we have to work at breaking the cycle. Gratitude helps us to shift perspective and open up our minds, allowing us to disentangle ourselves from negative thoughts.

Findings suggest that the effects of practicing gratitude are long lasting. The feeling of happiness that comes from appreciation may help train the brain to be more sensitive to the experience of gratitude. Gratitude appears to actually rewire our brain so we're better able to deal with adversity–both in the present moment and also to build reserves we can draw on down the road.

<u>Why practice gratitude meditation</u>? Many social psychologists believes that gratitude isn't our default setting. For survival purposes, humans were designed with instincts sensitive to the merest whiff of anything amiss. Our ancestors were hard-wired- not so much to appreciate a magnificent sunset, but to scan for a shadowy presence that could show danger.

Psychologists think this tendency to live more fully in our negative emotions rather than in our positive ones is an inherited evolutionary predisposition.

To shift our focus takes a little effort. And, as with many meditations, the more we practice it, the easier and more natural it becomes. The duration of your meditation is not important; what matters is consistency, which is key. Whether it's a few minutes each day, or once a week, the more appreciative moments we create for ourselves and the more we make a habit of giving thanks, the more we reap the benefits.

Chapter 6: Meditation For Stress

Life can be stressful, and stress can have serious repercussions on our health. At one time or another, many of us will have experienced that sense of being overwhelmed, as if everything were too much. Sometimes, simply taking time to pause and rest the mind can be enough to feel better in the moment, so before going any further, here's a quick exercise to help distance yourself from stressful thoughts right away.

Most people view stress as a threat to them. They think that stress is something they should avoid. But the individuals who grow most are the ones who look at the stress as a challenge.

<u>Stress–buster</u>. Meditation has been scientifically proven to help alleviate stress after just eight weeks of a regular practice. Many studies have shown that meditation is an effective stress-management tool, ultimately reprogramming the brain if meditators end up with more capacity to manage stress.

In training the mind to be more open and less reactive, we are better able to cope when life's stressors- in career, family, relationship, college, finances, even traffic–start accumulating, But before diving into how meditation combats stress, we first need to understand what stress does to the body.

<u>Physical effects of stress</u>. Physiologically, stress triggers the autonomic nervous system, leading to a spike in the release of epinephrine and cortisol–the "stress hormones". Too much epinephrine can increase the risk of heart attacks and strokes; too much cortisol can affect our health–increasing blood sugar levels, suppressing the immune system, and constricting blood vessels.

When these hormones are released into the bloodstream, the liver produces more glucose, which is what provides the energy to activate our fight-or-flight mechanism. We are hard-wired to spring into reaction mode each time this happens, causing an increase in blood pressure, heart rate, and cholesterol levels, all of which disrupts our immune system, energy levels, and sleep. Too much epinephrine can increase the risk of heart attacks and strokes; too much cortisol can increase blood sugar levels and constrict blood vessels.

Everyone's experience of stress is, of course, different. The extent of our stress largely depends on the demands placed on us and the responsibility we shoulder, and each of us should be familiar with how stress affects us, whether it's tension in the muscles, tightness in the chest, headaches, fatigue, insomnia, nausea, or dizziness to name a few of the symptoms.

We meditate to counter the "stress response" with the "relaxation response," leading to a decrease in blood pressure, heart rate, and oxygen consumption. It also creates a more gradual change in the brain, which is where meditation really works its magic. So through meditation, we are increasing our capacity to manage stress and be more aware. And so the more we meditate, the more we build this mental resilience.

There are, of course, other options available for stress-management, and many of these other tools—such as physical exercise, breathing techniques, and hypnosis—can help us at the moment. But for seeing a long-term reduction in stress, and when we meditate consistently on a daily basis for at least eight weeks, the science shows that meditation is an effective intervention capable of altering the physical anatomy of the brain, with as little input as 10 minutes a day.

Reframing stress. Rather than being caught up in our stress, meditation teaches us to become the observers of certain mental patterns and, therefore, become less physically affected by them.

<u>Good stress/bad stress</u>. Meditation isn't about eliminating stress; it's about managing it. A lot of that boils down to how we perceive stress. By altering our mindset, we can lessen the implications on our mental and physical health.

Stress often gets a bad rap which is perhaps undeserved. Think where we would be, for example, if we didn't have the distress signal that makes us flee from danger. Or if we didn't feel pressed to finish a project or homework on time. Some people even thrive in high-pressure careers, feeling completely in control in the fast lane and totally stressed out when things slow down. So the degrees of stress can differ from person to person. Nevertheless, good experiences in our best interest will still bring stress. There's no avoiding it.

Our appraisal of pressured situations can actually affect the level of distress we associate with a certain event. But, looking at this through the lens of mindfulness, it is possible to soften the way we perceive stress and relate to it in a more accepting way.

Chapter 7: How you can do stress management

Stress is a feeling of emotional or physical tension. It can come from any event or thought that makes you feel frustrated, angry or nervous. Stress is your body's reaction to a challenge or demand. In short bursts, stress can be positive, such as when it helps you avoid danger or meet a deadline.

Stress is the body's reaction to any change that requires a change or response. The body reacts to these changes with physical, mental and emotional responses. Stress is a normal part of life.

What are the causes of stress?

1. Being under lots of pressure.
2. Facing big changes.
3. Worrying about something.
4. Not having much or any control over the outcome of a situation.
5. Having responsibilities that you're finding overwhelming.
6. Not having enough work, activities or change in your life.
7. Times of uncertainty.
8. Over thinking.
9. Do not express to anyone.

Is stress good or bad?

Stress is key for survival, but too much stress can be detrimental. Emotional stress that stays around for weeks or months can weaken the immune system and cause high blood pressure, fatigue, depression, anxiety and even heart disease. In particular, too much epinephrine can be harmful to your heart.

Stress Management. Stress management is a wide spectrum of techniques and psychotherapies aimed at controlling a person's level of stress, especially chronic stress, usually for the purpose of and for the motive of improving everyday functioning.

Stress management techniques. Take a 10-minute walk. According to a few experts, if you take a walk it will help reduce endorphins in the system that cause stress. Practice mindfulness. Learning to focus on your breathing can help you reduce stress. Create an exercise habit. Write a reflection journal. Organize yourself.

How to relieve stress?

Exercise. Exercise is one of the most important things you can do to combat stress.

<u>Consider supplements.</u> Several supplements promote stress and anxiety reduction.

- Light a candle.
- Reduce your caffeine intake.
- Write it down.
- Chew Gum.
- Spend time with friends and family.
- Laugh.
- How to relax?
- Take slow, deep breaths. Or try other breathing exercises for relaxation.
- Soak in a warm bath.
- Listen to soothing music.

<u>Practice mindful meditation.</u> The goal of mindful meditation is to focus your attention on things that are happening right now in the present moment.

- Write things in your diary.
- Use guided imagery.

Chapter 8: How To Recover From Being Cheated On

Being cheated on by someone we love and care for is a horrendous experience that many of us have had to go through. What do you do to get past such heartache? How do you get recover from being cheated on? Sara Russell writes about five common responses to being cheated on and the four important things that will help you heal.

Sara Russell is a skill for change coach from a Radical Lineage, a Qi Gong instructor, and a Relationship Anarchist in the Santa Cruz Mountains, who helps her clients analyze behaviors, relationships, systems, and transactions to see where old habits are no longer serving them.

She guides them in cultivating awareness of where they have power, how to use it, and how to create spaciousness to accept where they are powerless. Finally, Sara teaches radical self-love-bringing compassion to all the above work, because change is hard, and being in a body is hard, and we don't have to do it alone.

I knew what I was supposed to do if I ever got cheated on: quit the relationship, socially shame my ex, and walk away with my head held high in self-righteous confidence that I wouldn't be treated that way, and never look back. But when I found out I'd been cheated on, I didn't get out. I felt turned inside-out and upside-down. Sure, I had my suspicions. I had them in my previous relationships, too. Little things didn't add up– somebody wouldn't be where they said they would be, or a "friend" would feel a little too charged but it was nothing overt, just enough to make you question whether something was going on or wonder if you were crazy.

I thought I needed to keep track of such things, that it was my job to protect myself from people lying to me, and if I maintained a heightened sense of vigilance, I could protect myself from the heartbreak of an infidelity. I could get out before something terrible happened.

But when I actually found out, I was blind-sided. My partner had offered me so many reassurances, given so explanations that I was all too ready to believe, because the alternative felt too awful. Sometimes, they would even guilt me for over-reacting, and ask me, "Why can't you just let us be happy"?

Faced with the infidelity, I didn't feel certain of what to do. Instead, I felt paralyzed by my confusion. How did this happen? Why did this happen? How can I fix this awful feeling? Am I broken now? Will I ever be able to trust a partner again?

How can I recover from being cheated on by someone I love?

Common Responses to being cheated on. When we learn that someone has acted unilaterally, without our consent, in a way that breaks trust, and harms our emotional, mental responses include:

1. **Fighting**. Persecuting our partner and trying to take control of the situation.

2. **Ignoring**. Acting like it didn't happen.

3. **Giving In**. Giving up what we want and need and tolerating how someone treats us.

4. **Negotiating**. Attempting to figure out a way to change the behavior.

5. **Taking Collective Action**. Soliciting support from our allies to help us escape a situation that is oppressing us.

You may cycle through these responses, hoping for a way to relieve your distress and recover from being cheated on.

There's no right answer, and the uniqueness of your context will determine your path towards healing.

<u>Take your Time</u>. The journey toward healing begins with taking care of yourself. You need time to go through everything you are feeling. It's tempting to want to continuously process what happened. There is an urgency in our bodies to figure out a solution to ease the almost unbearable level of agitation in our bodies.

This desire to act with immediacy makes sense (who wants to feel terrible for any amount of time?) but acting quickly doesn't produce satisfying, sustainable results. Instead, you need to give yourself time to feel all the messy, ever-changing, ever-evolving feelings that come up for you. Get clear on how you are actually feeling, and not how you wish or think you should be feeling.

<u>Take Space</u>. It's best to do the heavy work of grieving, raging, and accepting away from the source of your trigger. That means a period of no contact with the person who hurt you. It's too easy to get re-triggered, or be influenced by someone who has an agenda for you—someone who has shown they will prioritize their wants of an honest, transparent conversation with you. While you are taking space, name all the hard, heavy, complex, and sometimes contradictory things you are feeling: sad, hurt, angry, confused, hopeless, but maybe also the loneliness of missing your partner, and longing for love and connection.

It's a confusing storm, but it will pass with greater ease if you can hold the full truth of your narrative rather than trying to oversimplify it for quick and easy answers.

Recover from being cheated on Tip -1 Build trust in yourself.

Before doing the work of trusting another person, it's important you trust yourself. Be sincere with yourself about what you are feeling, and what you want. Take care of yourself- don't deplete yourself to the point of exhaustion because of somebody else's behaviors or needs. Teach your body, heart, and mind that you value ease and peace, not just effort and grinding through painful experiences, and that your well-being matters.

Make sure you have the time, energy, and resources you need to show up for yourself. Learn how to self-regulate and self soothe-don't rely on your partner to fix this for you. Cover your basics: try to get enough sleep, water, and nourishing foods. Do those things that make you feel centered, happy, creative, calm and inspired to get back the energy you lost from dealing with your heartache.

Recover from being cheated on Tip-2 Stop reliving the hurt

Resist the urge to relive the painful realizations, conversations and experiences that took place. You'll want to go back over everything that happened, to find clear answers, or to make sense of it all. Something awful and heartbreaking happened, and there are no quick and easy fixes.

Your job is not to go through with a fine-tooth comb and find every mistake and wrong move everybody made. Instead, create within yourself a big enough container to hold the entire messy complexity of what you are experiencing, and know that you are still okay. Even though it really sucks.

Recover from being cheated on Tip-3 Know that it's not about you

How someone treats you be not about you. It's about their stories, about themselves, and the world, and how they believe things should be.

Your self-worth is not determined by what anyone else thinks or does. You decide what works for you, and what doesn't. You give away what power you have when you let somebody else tell the story of your worth. What happened to you is painful and heartbreaking. It is hard enough, without adding shame and pressure on yourself to make yourself responsible for someone else's bad behavior.

Recover from being cheated on Tip 4 What's next

We so desperately want there to be a way to fix what happened, but it's time to accept the unacceptable and hold the truth of what is. Once you've recovered, you can decide- what are your minimum standards, and what are your boundaries? What are deal breakers for you? What is a natural consequence of someone else's behavior falling below your minimum standard, or crossing your boundaries?

Forgive yourself for trusting someone who didn't deserve your trust. Forgive yourself for what you didn't know. Forgive yourself for what you suspected but ignored because it was easier, or because you loved your partner so much.

Once you can forgive yourself, it's much easier to forgive the other person. That doesn't mean they still have a place in your life. You get to decide what you need and want.

Chapter 9: Finding Moderation And Balance In Life

You might have heard that moderation is essential for a healthy, happy lifestyle and blissful life. Buddhists and Stoics alike have been explaining for millennia how maintaining balance in your life is the key to meaning and tranquility. Finding the right equilibrium can be difficult. However, with diligent, consistent effort, you can find the right amount of moderation and balance in every aspect of your life.

Finding Balance And Moderation At Work

Finding the right balance at work can be tricky. The constant pressure to perform may encourage you to work longer and longer hours, afraid you won't be able to set yourself apart. It's easy to fall into burnout, resenting your job yet working around the clock out of fear.

While working too much can be a serious problem, so can slacking off. If you want to excel in your profession and enjoy decades of success, you must do more than the bare minimum. To increase your chances of rising in your career, you must put in the work required to contribute creatively to your organization.

Finding balance can take time, and you'll swing between extremes before you get the hang of it. I've had 80- hour weeks where I was running on fumes. I've also had months where I was convinced that living an ultra- minimalist lifestyle and working as little as possible was the answer. Now, I believe a happy medium-the middle way- is the best course of action.

Finding Balance And Moderation In Health

When it comes to the gym–track, yoga mat, etc.,–finding a happy medium helps promote a long, healthy life. Sitting on your couch all day is a sure way to poor health. Overexerting yourself can lead to over training and burnout. Sometimes, extreme exercise may also carry cardiovascular risks.

Everything in moderation, including moderation while balance and moderation are useful tools in a healthy life, sometimes you might want to get a little extreme.

None of these times in my life were exercised in moderation. Every once in a while, if you have sights set on a lofty goal, you might need to take a break from moderation and put forth your very best effort. Once you've accomplished your goal, prioritize the areas of your life you may have neglected while pursuing the goal and return in life? (Michael Bjorn Huseby)

Chapter 10: 7 Self-Care Hacks For When You're Overwhelmed

I often need to remind myself that the only thing in the world I can control is me. Luckily, there is great power in always knowing I am in control of how I respond to all the overwhelming things happening around me. Keeping a routine is helpful for some people. I have several friends and clients who have been using the extra time at home, to clean, declutter, organize, and remodel their homes. Having control over your personal space can really give you a sense of authority in your life.

Personally, I took on a new skill. I spent the summer getting my yoga teacher certification online, and now I am learning to play the ukulele. Having something interesting and novel to do when I get overwhelmed is a great way to support myself. Yoga and music-making are ideal outlets for my self-care because not only do they distract from the chaos in the world, but they also allow me to have a cathartic physical and emotional release.

Find Inner Peace With These Self-Care Hacks (Heidi Green)

I'm taking a lot of walks and enjoying time outdoors. Even if you live somewhere colder, getting outside and being in nature can be very grounding. Being mindful of all your sensory experiences, such as what you see, hear, smell, physically feel, or even taste can add an extra grounding benefit.

Journaling and meditating more frequently lately and find both very helpful. Journaling allows me to get my thoughts and feelings out of my head and onto paper. It also creates an opportunity for me to validate myself and my experiences. I've been doing the loving kindness meditate on daily and offering myself lots of self-love and self-compassion in my meditation practice. This helps me feel kinder, gentler, and or of myself, others, and my situation. Here are the seven self-care:

- Control what you can.
- Keep a routine.
- Organize your space.
- Learn a new skill.
- Connect with nature.
- Journal.
- Meditate.

Chapter 11: How To Change Your Beliefs With Affirmations

I've found that sometimes I need to trick my mind into changing my beliefs. While there are endless ways to do this, one, in particular, has worked well for me, incorporating affirmations into my daily life has helped change my beliefs more habitually. And when you alter your beliefs, especially when it comes to what you think about yourself, life gets a lot better.

What are affirmations? In the simplest of terms, affirmations are just statements. We are affirmations all day long. Unfortunately, most of them are negative. "I don't feel well," "I'm just not any good at this," and "I feel so frustrated" are all examples of negative affirmations.

Most of us have thought or said aloud statements like this for most of our adult life. They are ingrained in our minds (and beliefs). But there are simple ways to change what you tell yourself. Focusing on bringing positive affirmations into your life, using one simple technique, makes a big difference.

How to change your beliefs by making positive affirmations part of your life

As I mentioned earlier, affirmations become habits. If you say something over and over, it's likely to stick. Think about when you repeat a behavior several times. You get better at it, right? The same thing goes for affirmations, whether they are positive or negative.

To make your affirmations or statements more positive, try setting alarms on your phone. In the description box, add a positive affirmation about yourself. "I do amazing work for my company," "I love being me," and "I am smart" are three you want to improve in, use an affirmation to help you.

Let's say you aren't great with numbers but want to improve your finances. Your belief is probably that you're not good with math. Instead of continuing to focus on your weakness, flip the statement around and say, "I'm improving my finances every day". This allows you to take a negative statement and turn it into a positive affirmation.

Watch as your beliefs change. Remember, incorporating more positive affirmations into your life doesn't have to be hard. Every time my alarm goes off on my phone, and I see a positive affirmation pop up, I smile. It truly changes the way my day goes, and my overall outlook on life.

Chapter 12: The Magical 7 Ways To Program The Subconscious Mind

We have two types of mind that is a conscious mind and subconscious minds controls our logical thinking, critical thinking, short-term memory etc., and subconscious mind controls long-term memory, intuition power, imagination, feelings and it doesn't have any logical thinking.

Let's talk about the 7 ways to program the subconscious mind:

1. **Teenage that is 4 to 5 years old**. The age between 4 to 5 years, the conscious mind was not developed completely, so it doesn't give any logic. So what we learn from others is directly inserted in our subconscious mind, and then it had made a belief system.

2. **Repetition**. When we think of our dream, goals repeatedly then it enters in our subconscious mind then the subconscious mind manifests the particular thing.

3. **Emotion**. When we think a thing with lots of emotions, feelings, then it directly enters to our subconscious mind.

4. **Hypnosis**. Hypnosis is the way where you directly enter anything you want into your subconscious mind. You can make self -hypnosis or by a person who knows the details about hypnosis. In this method our conscious mind distract and then all the commands said by you or by hypnotist is enters to subconscious mind.

5. **Logic**. When you give some logic about your thinking, then your conscious mind accepts the thinking and transfers it to the subconscious mind and then it becomes a part of your belief system.

6. **Significant figure**. Significant figure means who you believe the most may be your father, mother, sister, brother or friends or relatives. When they say something about you, then your subconscious mind accepts the thing and believe on those things. Those things are directly enters to your subconscious mind.

7. **Sensory rich language**. Sensory rich language means when a person is saying about some situations or something else then audios, images and some visualization are created in your mind then you can feel the situation or you can say that you are present in that situation in that particular time but that is not real, you imagine that situation and this enters your subconscious mind.

Chapter 13: How Does Your Body And Mind Benefit From A Good Sleep?

One of the oddest things we do every day is sleep. The average adult will spend 36% of his life. We have switched from the vibrant, reflective and active creatures, we are in the summer to a peaceful state of winter resting for one-third of our time on Earth.

Sleep can decrease anxiety. If you didn't get enough nap, it can react by producing a high level of stress hormones, which are a natural result of today's fast-paced lifestyles. A deep and regular nap can help limit this.

Sleep increases your memory. Ever noticed that when you're exhausted, it's harder to memorize things? This is your brain informing you it's not getting sufficient sleep. When you rest well, your body may relax, but your brain is busy arranging and storing memories. So getting more quality sleep will help you keep and process things better.

Sleep lower's your blood pressure. Higher blood pressure increases your risks of heart attacks and strokes, but getting a lot of restful sleep helps a regular state of relaxation that can help decrease blood pressure and regularly keep it under check.

<u>Sleep can help you maintain your weight</u>. Sadly, sleep won't instantly make you lose weight, but it can aid you keep it under check by controlling the hormones that influence you craving and lowering your needs for high-calorie foods.

For the mind, REM sleep is slow for the body. During most sleep periods, the brain is relatively calm, but your brain comes alive during REM. REM sleep is when the brain dreams of knowledge and re-organizes it. During this stage your brain eliminates any irrelevant information, improves your memory by comparing the last 24 hours of experiences with previous experiences and encourages neural developed and learning. The body will increase temperatures, blood pressure and heart rates will rise. Your body barely moves through all this movement. The REM phase usually happens about 3 to 5 times a night in brief explosions.

A study performed on the Stanford basketball players considers the effect of sleep on physical performance. The players slept at least ten hours' per night during this study (compared to their typical 8 hours). The investigators measured the accuracy and pace of basketball players during five weeks of extended sleep in relation to their previous rates. The shooting percentage of three points increased 9.2%. And when sprinting 80 meters, the players were 0.6 seconds quicker.

Slow wave sleep helps you recover when your place heavy physical demands on your body. Your brain will be happy the whole day by following these rule.

Chapter 14: The Best Yoga Techniques For A Blissful Life

The best procedure for any individual thinking about taking up Yoga isn't to consider however to focus—on how yoga and its methods are growing into an overall pestilence where yoga practices are helping to ail patients and other people who look for genuine feelings of serenity.

Understanding Yoga is much less confounded than you could envision, however, if you are considering taking up the training, there are some yoga methods you should know about and apply throughout the activity.

Yoga is, without uncertainty, possibly the best activities performed to now in assisting individuals with the remaining fit as a fiddle and to stay in shape and sound. You will be astonished how yoga finds a way that it can be practiced anyplace and anytime.

Individuals are taking increasingly more interest in keeping their wellness levels at a point where they are gaining a better way of life, and this is all gratitude to yoga. Yoga methods are useful in adjusting your body organs. Muscles, joints, organs, tissues are additionally kept up by certain procedures of Yoga.

There are five yoga methods that you may appreciate, including in your exercise. They are contemplation, unwinding, profound breathing, stance, and development of the joints. All of this yoga capacities have their strategy. Also called the sandhichalana, is the place where the development of joints becomes an integral factor.

This is performed and exclusively coordinated by yoga adherents towards facilitating the joints. Joints are liberated from firmness by going through and rehearsing full developments, which comprise hand neck and lower appendage developments.

A yoga method behind the unwinding exercise is to have the option to develop your focus design, which plans to help deflect any impedance that stands out for you with no problem.

The Hong-Sau is another method used, which helps you further in zeroing in on the disguised forces of focus. This is an incredible yoga schedule that can help you fight any interfering aggravations while simultaneously furnishing you with a loose and quiet inclination within.

Each to their own on what exercise to practice yet possibly the most mainstream is the Aum (Oom) strategy, which extends blissfulness long ways past any constraints that your body and brain make. By maintaining an uninterrupted meditation, you gain contentment.

A large number of the strategies referenced won't be fitting for the fledgling, so guidance from a yoga expert would be your best method. Make sure to pose inquiries on various sorts of yoga and the procedures, this will assist you to decide which one to take up.

Look at it for yourself, come to a nearby class in your general vicinity, and watch exactly the number of individuals who are leaving you behind in guaranteeing better body blissfulness and a positive way to deal with life.

Chapter 15: How To Keep Your Brain Healthy

Health is a major issue in the present times when the world is still recovering from the deadly attack of a pandemic. Building strong immunity is of utmost importance to protect oneself from any kind of disease. Proper diet should've accompanied by a healthy lifestyle to keep diseases at bay. Going to a gym is the most popular option among urban people.

Cardio and weight exercises produce positive effects in many ways. But what about the "headquarter of the body"? The dark side of the modern lifestyle is that we are making our brains idle and weak. Sticking to the phone, captured in the world of you tube videos, giving up reading habits, no time to think, are making our brains idle and weak. We have no time for that part of the body that controls everything. Sad!!! We think we are tech savvy, but we are actually becoming slaves of technology. We need a calculator to add four items.

Here are three games that act as muscle building workouts for the brain. These games can be played anytime, at any place, and there is no need to spend a penny. It just needs few moments. Schulte Table: This is a number game

like Sudoku and has been proven to be booster
work out for the brain.

20	2	16	9	18
12	24	17	14	1
19	21	10	15	5
22	4	8	3	13
25	13	7	6	11

Spending few moments regularly on this game
can improve peripheral vision, attention, and
visual reception.

Hand Gestures: This is a miraculous game
that improves the coordination capability of the
brain. This workout increases alertness. The
game involves interchanging the gestures of the
left and right hand quickly. For example, right
hand of left hand thumbs up, then vice versa, but
changing the signs as fast as possible.

Multicolor text: This is another fun game that
makes the brain sweat and increases response
time, activeness, and alertness of the brain. The
trick is to read the color, not the text. Regular
practice with this game can make the brain more
alert and active.

Reading a book or text loudly. This is a
practice mostly known to be religious is very
effective in enhancing memory. Hearing one's

own voice has been very effective in exciting the memory cells of the brain.

Interchanging Hands. Most of us use our right hand for performing almost all kinds of jobs. It has been scientifically proved that occasional changing of hands, like trying to write with left hand, increases the responsiveness of the brain. Interchanging of hands occasionally stimulates the locomotive part of the brain and gathers the neurons closely.

Aerobic exercises. Doing aerobic exercises at least three days a week improves blood circulation and oxygen supply to the brain which rejuvenates the brain cells and improves brain activity. Aerobic workouts help remove lumps in brain and open clots. Thus refreshes the brain and gives the cells a new life.

Passive memory training. Observing four to five details of the people and place that we observe on roads or public places.

Chapter 16: How To Get Happiness And Success Through Intrinsic Motivation

"Extrinsic motivation is of no use without intrinsic motivation and once you have intrinsic motivation, you may not need extrinsic motivation" Eva Bhinde

Have you ever sung a song when alone, have you ever painted a picture with engrossment? Or have you ever played cricket without caring about the time? How did you feel? I am sure you would remember these moments with a big smile on your face. That is something inner motivation.

There are two kinds of motivation: first is inner or intrinsic motivation and the other is external motivation.

Intrinsic motivation (from within)	Extrinsic motivation (from outside)
Autonomy	Compensation
Mastery	Punishment
Purpose	Reward

External motivation is inspired by the rewards that others offer. We work for something like money, status, praise, rewards, etc. Intrinsic motivation is different. It is not attracted by any outside rewards. It is an internal business. It is an act with no obvious external rewards. You do it just because you love to do it. You enjoy doing it. You neither have the pressure of doing with excellence nor any deadlines to follow, neither you will get any rewards nor any incentives. You do it for your own self. It is your psychological need.

Your action may look the same, but the intention for doing the activity is completely different. You read a book to clear the exam that is external motivation, but you read out of interest is internal motivation. You work to get money is external motivation, but you work because you enjoy working is internal motivation. In simple words, external motivation raises your lifestyle but internal motivation raises your life.

External motivation is something that is offered from the outside. Like your boss may promote you if you do your work in time but is someone has the power to motivate you, he also has the power to demotivate you. That means your key of inspiration, motivation or happiness lies in others' hands. Do not let your happiness go into others' hands. Inspiration should come from inside. When you are inspired by the inside, no one dared to demotivate you. Your inner motivation will create a strong desire to work, your strong desire will make a firm determination, your firm determination will put you in immense efforts and immense efforts will bring great success. That is the power of inner motivation.

Many times, we underestimate this power. We must develop the quality of inner motivation. Give yourself a strong reason. The strong reason is your "Big why". This is the real purpose of your activity. You must convince your intellect of the benefits of sticking to that activity or you must convince your intellect of the harms of not sticking to it. Your intellect will help to develop your inner motivation.

This story will tell you the importance of the power of why and how intellect helps to develop inner motivation. There was a King who had appointed a servant. One day the King caught him stealing some money. The King got angry and put him on a sentence of death. Somehow King thought of playing sword war with the servant. He told the servant. "Let's do a war, If I win, I'll kill you with my sword, but if at all you win, I'll release you from your punishment". Everyone was sure that the King would win hands down, but servant fought so furiously that the King had to stop the war and released him.

King was very surprised by the servant's fight as he had never lifted a sword in his hands ever in his lifetime. He asked one of his intelligent ministers. The reason is very obvious. You were fighting just to "play" but he had a strong reason to fight. He had "Big Why" to fight that made him win. Conviction of his intellect gave him that success.

When people are inner motivated, they are:

<u>More creative</u>. They don't have any pressure of work. They have free choice to work upon. More successful: Internally motivated people do not discourage by external demotivation. In fact, they don't focus on results; they enjoy the process with no tension, which makes them more successful.

<u>More committed and persistent</u>. Inner motivation is not driven by any external rewards, people do it for their own happiness, and since they are more committed and more persistent.

<u>More satisfied.</u> People enjoy the work they do and find real satisfaction out of it.

The following are some things you can do to develop inner motivation:

- Don't focus on external rewards. Enjoy the process.

- Keep on improving on the task or focus on mastering the skill.

- Help others expecting nothing in return.

- Make a list of the things you love to do and take out time to do them.

- Challenge yourself to do some activities and accomplish them.

- Inner motivation will never discourage you, it will give you the right direction and real purpose in life. Because it is very important to know "why we do, what we do".

Chapter 17: Why Rich People Are Unhappy?

Today, all over the world, people are so sad even having all the properties. Many rich people are committing suicide all over the world. During the COVID-19, so many people committed suicide. Why? It's because they were not happy and confident about life. They thought that the crisis will finish them. They were in depression because of hard times. This is because they never know the meditation. They never read their own book of life.

If we look back decidedly, we find that there is no inner peace and stability.

Osho wants to make a new man who is prosperous; able to use all the modern facilities and travel towards in the inner being; the world of Buddha.

Zorba the Buddha is a complete man who is rich inwardly and outwardly. The man who travels from money to meditation lives a complete life.

Money and meditation are the inseparable parts of the same coin. Both money and meditation are equally important in life. But people are concern with money only.

Connecting money to meditate. Before Osho's arrival, money and meditation used to be taken as opponent. There was a belief that both can't go together. There was practice that money must be avoided to get in meditation. This means one needs to give up all the worldly pleasures to be spiritual. Osho denied it and established the facts that money and meditation are interdependent. They need for each other. This is the biggest lesson by Osho.

We have seen that Osho used to wear a diamond hat. He had hundreds of Rolls Royce when he was in America. In those days, even the richest Americans also didn't have such cars. Despite having all these worldly facilities, Osho moved ahead, being powerful with his spiritual activities.

The main thing is we must not just stock in the world with such pleasures. Enjoy all the facilities and worldly things available for you and don't forget meditation. He says 'no meditation, no life, know meditation, know life'.

If we understood the teaching of Osho, we become a new man who has prosperity in the outer world and never ending pleasure in the inner world.

Chapter 18: Why Is Mindfulness Popular In The World?

Mindfulness is the best practice to sharpen awareness. Awareness plays an important and central role in human life. The man becomes peaceful and successful if he is aware of him and his every activity. The awareness doesn't refer to the information about something: it is the state of 'knowing' about oneself and the activities by an individual.

What is mindfulness? In recent days, mindfulness has been so much popular all over the world. Mainly, the western world is making a massive practice of mindfulness. Mindfulness is the best practice to sharpen awareness. We sit, eat, walk, speak, wear a dress and do many things every day. Every day, we do multifarious activities. If we do all these things 'knowingly' (with full awareness) then it becomes mindfulness.

Mindfulness is the practice of being in present. Every day, we do many works knowingly and unknowingly. We sit to eat, but our mind goes somewhere else. Body and mind are not together. Where there is a body, there is no mind. And where there is mind there is nobody. The body and mind must be in together, but there is a dichotomy which creates discomfort.

We eat food, but there is no attention in every morsel of rice. Some people do not even know the taste of the food they have eaten. People are eating food as if they are putting something in a container; unconsciously. The same thing is happening everywhere.

Mindfulness asks to bring awareness (knowingness) in doing all kinds of activities. We must know what we are doing.

If you are walking: you must know every step. You are eating then must know the complete eating phenomena. All activities must be done being fully aware.

People say that mindfulness and meditation are the same. They say mindfulness is meditation. Indeed, there is a vast gap between mindfulness and meditation.

Meditation is the journey from mind to no-mind state; from thoughtfulness to thoughtlessness. But mindfulness is just awareness of all the activities we do every day. Mindfulness happens in mind, or there is the role of the mind. Meditation happens beyond the mind.

How to practice mindfulness? Mindfulness is the best practice to sharpen awareness in everything we do daily. Therefore, we must know how to practice it in life.

There are no hard and fast rules to practice mindfulness. You can make your plan as per your wish. However, I will suggest the most common and effective ways of practicing mindfulness. There are six effective ways:

- Breathing Awareness.
- Walking Awareness.
- Eating Awareness.
- Talking Awareness.
- Sitting Awareness.
- Wearing Awareness.

Every day we do many works so often. Among them, let's practice awareness in doing the above activities.

Breathing awareness. We are breathing all the time. Observe breathing. Pay attention to every inhale and exhale. Find out how breathing is doing in and out in the body. Gradually, we will know our every breathing.

Walking awareness. Every day we walk around, but we don't pay attention to how we are walking. Now, let's pay attention to every walking. Observe at every pace- in every step.

You can ancient practice taking every step in full awareness.

Eating awareness. We are eating most of the time but like machines. Now, practice eating with full attention. Try to catch the taste of the food. Understand how much you eat. We will improve eating quality with awareness.

Talking awareness. Every time we are talking with someone. Sometimes, we talk to each other for a long hour. We hurt people by talking as well. Sometimes, we waste time for meaningless things, but we don't know about it because there is no awareness. Now, everyone can practice talking with full awareness. Gradually, talking becomes sweet with awareness.

Sitting awareness. Likewise, pay attention to sitting postures. We must fully know sitting. Where are you sitting? How are you sitting? Pay attention to all these activities. This practice will make our sitting perfect and healthy.

Wearing awareness. In the same way, every day we wear many clothes. Now we need to practice knowing the color, size, textures and many more about the clothes that we wear.

When we make intensive attention in doing activities, gradually we do thing naturally. This will make different feeling in us. The productivity of daily work will be increased in a great amount.

These simple practices will decidedly help us make a great difference in our life.

What are the major benefits of mindfulness? There are many benefits of mindfulness so that people around the world are practicing it. Let's talk about a few major benefits;

- Improves focusing and observation power.
- Minimize errors in daily life.
- Become more peaceful mentally.
- Become successful in work.

The first thing is mindfulness increases a lot of power in observation and focusing the thing. People become a keen observer. They wholeheartedly focus on work or anything they are doing which bring outstanding success in life.

We commit many errors while doing multifarious works in daily life. Mindfulness helps to minimize the errors in work because we become fully focus on work. There is no chance of doing a mistake as we realize doing works.

One of the biggest problems in man's life is to become restless. People are full of tension. There is no patience in them because people do works carelessly without awareness. When we practice mindfulness, gradually we realize all the activities which make man peaceful. Mentally we become peaceful.

Similarly, mindfulness brings a lot of success in life. We know that people do practice mindfulness for peace and prosperity. If there is a full awareness in doing all the daily activities, we become successful.

Hence, mindfulness is the best practice to sharpen awareness in daily life, which helps to make a blissful life ahead.

Chapter 19: 2 Inseparable Sides Of Blissful Life

Blissful life is the only desire of a man

Happiness is the ultimate destination for the lives of nearly 8 billion people on this planet. Suppose you want to be a doctor, a pilot, an engineer, or a lawyer and became. Also, you earn a name and money. You have successfully reached your goal. What do you want now? Of course, you want happiness, don't you? Therefore, all human beings have the ultimate and common goal of life: happiness.

In fact, most people's desire to live a blissful life has not been fulfilled. They have family, children, wealth, honor, position, beautiful body, everything, but no happiness. Why are people sad despite having everything? You know that the number of sad people on this earth is terrifically increasing day by day. Please read the proven data below:

- Over 264 million people yearly suffer from depression.
- Close to 800,000 people commit suicide yearly.
- 20% of people around the world are sleep deprived.

- Worldwide gun deaths reach 250,000 yearly.
- Marriage is declining, single is increasing.
- The divorce rate is also increasing in some countries.
- Global estimates published by WHO indicate that about 1 in 3 (35%) of women worldwide have experienced either physical or sexual intimate partner violence in their lifetime.

Besides this, the world is witnessing much different violence every day. Even in a country with rich and educated people, the monstrosity of murder and violence can be seen rising.

There can be many reasons behind these bitter facts, but the main reason is people's unhappiness. We understand that only the unhappy person becomes ready for any kind of violence.

Generally, different sorrows, sufferings, problems, pains, etc., gradually push people towards crime. And there is a strong possibility that he will commit a crime.

Being sad and happy has a great meaning and value in life. We must understand this and start a journey towards a blissful life.

Now we all need to understand something about how to move towards happiness, the only destination of life. Let's understand the science of a happy life.

Many people think that if I get all the things I need: a life partner, wealth, fame, then my life will be happier. However, this is not the case. Many rich and famous people have committed suicide. They are also frustrated. Therefore, it is necessary to understand blissfulness from the root. There are two main aspects of a blissful life: inner and outer world.

If we want happiness in life, we must have inner peace and outer progress. When we are complete and balance in both areas, we get the happiness we want. Nowadays, people are often just looking for progress outside. They have wealth, position, prestige but do not have peace in mind. This means simply there is no balance between the inner and the outer world. When we maintain a balance between inside and out, we become automatically happy.

What is the inner world? Man thinks and feels. Thoughts and feelings are constantly being produced in the mind. All the thinking and feeling happen in the inner world. These thoughts and feelings are also affected by the outside world. Under normal circumstances, the mind is not under human control. The mind is constantly thinking of good and bad things. According to science, 70,000 thoughts are produced in the human brain in 24 hours. They are more bad than good. If many thoughts come to mind uncontrollably, a person cannot sleep. Insomnia can start.

Since the mind is constantly producing thoughts, we need to understand this. We say that the most amazing thing is that a man thinks. Indeed, the man doesn't think. Thinking happens in man. This strange to listen but it is a bitter reality.

For the sake of conversation, I wrote earlier that man thinks. But the reality is just the opposite. Thoughts are being produced by the mind itself. If why do we think something bad? Tell me, please. You encounter many bad and negative thoughts every day. Did you think that on your own? Can you think something bad for you, yourself? None of us want to think badly about ourselves, but it happens.

When we see a sick person, in no time we think we may get sick in the same way. We don't want that, but it happens. Why? It's because the control of producing thought is not in our hands. It is in the hands of the mind. The mind is producing thoughts and emotions according to its own will. We are the servants of the mind. We are going wherever he takes us.

Everyone knows well that the things like cigarettes, alcohol, marijuana, hashish affect the body. They must be consumed. You know the reality that people are massively consuming all those dangerous things. Why don't people think of eating fruits instead? If people ate fruits and milk, it could cure the body. It would have been very good. However, this is not happening. Why is the mind only thinking badly?

Similarly, people don't want to be lazy, addicted, and criminals but they are becoming again? Can anyone mislead us if we don't want to? Absolutely not, the entire game is being led by our mind. We are going wherever our mind takes us as a puppy. Now, you may have a question. Can't we control the mind? Can't we make the mind a servant?

<u>We can control our minds</u>. We can be masters, not slaves of the mind. If we practice with confidence, the mind comes under our control. Let's talk about that.

First, it is necessary to understand the characteristics of the mind. And you have already understood something about it. The mind is fickle. It is always looking for something to eat. The mind keeps searching for something like a cat digging a tree to sharpen its claws. People's mind tries to flow downhill like water, it tries to be more attracted towards negative things. Once you understand this, the journey makes a beautiful inner world.

Since the mind is always searching for something, we react to unnecessary things and get into disputes. So try to observe any thoughts or feelings that come to mind. Do not retaliate or respond to any thought. As you were reading at home, the dog barked outside. Are you angry or upset? Do not respond as well. Observe your anger or irritation carefully. No comment at all.

Make the mind like a transparent wall so that what is penetrated from one side can come out from the other side. Mostly when something touches our mind, we stand like a wall and start reacting to it. Don't respond. Just observe it.

What do you do when you see the sky? You just look at the sky. You don't comment on the color, the clouds, or anything, do you? In the same way, just sit and observe the sky of the mind. The more you react, the more aggressive and restless your mind becomes. The mind goes out of your control. Therefore, no reaction, no comment: just witness all happenings of your mind. The most beautiful effort to control the mind is to be unresponsive.

Don't respond to anything? Respond when you need to, but you don't have to respond to the little things that happen every day. It only serves to provoke the mind.

Now, the thinking won't happen in you. You will think yourself like Buddha. We feel peace. We become stable. No more negative or harmful thoughts come in your mind. You become the master of your mind.

What is the outer world? We live in a society with a family. There is a relationship with people. Everyone works every day because they have a purpose in life. We have to become someone remarkable person in life.

Everybody needs to earn money and prestige, buy a car, a house, and get married. In fact, there are many things to be done in this world. And the most important thing is we want to live a long life. This is our outside world. This is how we move to the outer world.

Our outer world is built on in the composition of different components like family, health, wealth, education, dignity, relationships, and aim. We hover around them for outstanding success. In order to achieve our aim in life, we must be able to use all these components equally.

We need to understand the role of all the components from the kernel. If we didn't understand them well, we fail to use them as per our requirement, maintaining a perfect balance.

Our only goal in the outside world is to achieve success. In order to succeed in the field we want.

We must use the resources we have and the efforts we can make. We should always be able to use all the elements of our outer world: health, family, education, dignity, relationships, etc., consciously. Only then can we succeed. If we forget or undermine the role of these components and move on, it will lead to misery.

Most people in the world today are making the same mistake. In the name of making money, they are forgetting their health, family, and dignity and doing whatever they can. When we earns ample wealth, we may have nothing with our family, health, or dignity. This is often the most important mistake people make in the outside world. We need to acknowledge this.

Many people may have to work far away from their families and relatives. When we are busy with our own work, we should not forget none of our family, but many people forget their family. In the name of a busy schedule, they forget the family, which is the most important link of our outer world. This creates a selfish manner in them.

As long as you are physically strong in life, you can live alone, but as time goes by, it is necessary to be with someone. You need help, but there is no one with you. Who will help them? Therefore, we understand that all the time when you are in the world you must forget the importance of the components mentioned above. They have a great role in our life and success. It is better to understand the fact now and move forward.

After understanding the outer and the inner worlds of our life separately, we also need to understand the relationship between them for the blissful life. It's because we want happiness in life.

Success in any one world alone does not make a person happy. We must walk wisely in both worlds. It is necessary to work with equal importance in both worlds. Give both worlds an equal share for a happy life. These two worlds are like two banks of a river. When there are two sides, only the river of happiness flows smoothly. The two sides and water jointly make a river. We can't imagine the river without two sides.

Nobody can imagine a blissful life without the combination of two sides. The two sides (outer & inner world) jointly make a blissful life:

- Seek success in the outer world; seek peace in the inner world.

- Expose in the outer world; observe in the inner world.
- Enjoy the outer world, but when the time comes, return to the outer world.
- Enjoy the inner world, but when the time comes, return to the outer world.
- When there is a balance between the two worlds, there is a blissful life, if there is an imbalance, there is a sorrowful life.
- What to choose is in our hands. Let's choose a blissful life.

Finally, remember that there are two integral parts of our blissful life: the inner world and the outer.

Chapter 20: How To Control Anger Management

Usually, we all have a sense of angry, but having anger is not good. By this, we deprive our happiness, relationship, aim, education, etc. Though we can't avoid to anger, we can control. Here we enter how to control angry by the following things.

Don't think too much. Too much thinking leads to anger sometimes. We need to avoid this as much as possible because of keeping thinking about particularly the same one, then our brain will frustrate and become lazy by which we anger. And thinking should be in the surrounding of what we thinking about otherwise it is unused.

Reduce expectations. Expectations are unconquerable one to humans and which rises from desiring to something. Once we get it, we will be happy suppose it's not come to us we anger and become upset, disappointed, feeling anxious, shouting unnecessarily. So our duty is for control anger is to reduce expectations.

Be with children. As we know children are God and they don't have concerns, speak frankly, always be happy, quickly forget something we said about them. When we speak and play with them we forget about our angry, concerns, some little problems. Seeing children's smile is showing now we are in heaven and make happy. Their funny speech amusing and innocent habits are the major source to change our anger into delightful. When we take them into our hands, we realize God is not here or there instead of within our hands, not try to be with children while feeling not better.

Start read books. We all forget to anger when we read the books deeply. The reason is good books attract us and stimulate learn something new daily. Also, our brain nourishes by book reading and used to function the human part correctly and actively. When our brain with the good condition then we never fall into anger.

Writing on the paper. We can reduce our anger by sitting down for a while and writing our worries and the reason we are angry. It is only possible when we are angry with someone or if we need to reduce our anger and write our words and thoughts and understand them. It is enough to write our words into letters on a piece of paper to change our thoughts and reduce angrily.

Be alone a little of time. The best medicine to reduce anger is to sit in solitude for a while and think about yourself. The assurance of being alone can reveal many things about us and the things we do not know. When in solitude we should not be thinking that there is no one even ours otherwise think about how to stay with us, this is an important source to accomplish and reduce angrily?

<u>Watch great comedian videos</u>. By watching comedy videos we get to relieve stress, improvement of immunity, muscle relaxation, burns calories, simulate brains, good heart function, natural medicine to overcome stress. These leads to reduce our angry. Try above things for a happy life.

Conclusion

I hope you now have a better understanding of what your peaceful mind for a blissful life is, how it works and what a powerful weapon it can be when it comes to transforming your life. My challenge to you is to begin right now to put your positive mind to work for you... to reprogram it to help you achieve the life you truly desire. The way to begin is by following the approach outlined in chapter 1 to 20 of this book. And once again, I want to personally invite you to read my following books in series. I wish you every success and blissful life. To him be the glory and the power forever! (I Peter 4:11).

- Key To Happiness.
- Mindfulness For Entrepreneurs.

References

My knowledge and understanding of the Peaceful Mind For A Blissful Life have come from the study of numerous books, courses, and websites over a many years. While it would be impossible to list them all here, I would like to specifically acknowledge the following books/ or websites which have proven particularly helpful to me in developing my understanding of the peaceful mind for a blissful life and how it functions. The Book of Joy by The Dalai Lama, The Happiness Project by Gretchen Rubin, The Power of Meaning: Crafting A Life That Matters by Emily Esfahani Smith, How to Live More and Worry Less by Dale Carnegie, The Power of Subconscious Mind by Joseph Murphy, Headspace.com, A. Pawlowski, liveblissfull.com, Swellwomen.com.

Could You Please Leave A Review on the Book?

I'd love if you could leave a review about the book. Reviews may not matter to big-name authors; but it is a tremendous help for authors like me, who don't have much following. It help me to grow my readership by encouraging folks to take a chance on my books.

To put it straight – reviews are the life blood for any author.

Please leave your reviews in the book review page.

It will just take less than a minute of yours, but will tremendously help me to reach out to more people, so please leave your reviews happily.

Thank you for supporting my work and I'd love to see your review on the book for my happiness.

ABOUT THE BOOK

Are you thrilled, cheerful, and at **peace** with it? What you think of when you think of **happiness?** Is it a feeling you chase after but never quite reach, or a state of **mind** that you're able to tap into if you have the right resources? **Happiness** is a state of **mind**-an underlying sense of contentment, fulfillment, and satisfaction in life.

Here's the good news: the feeling is already there, readily accessible, often buried beneath layers of **thoughts and emotions**.

Today, all over the world, people are so sad even having all the properties. Many rich people are committing suicide all over the world. During COVID-19, so many people committed suicide. Why? It's because they were not **happy** and confident about life. They thought that the crisis will finish them. They were in depression because of hard times. This is because they never read their own book of life.

Mindfulness is the best practice to sharpen awareness. Awareness plays an important and control role in human life. The man becomes **peaceful** and successful if he is aware of him and his every activity.

You can enhance your life right away and make it **blissful**, purposeful and **happy**. All you need to do is identify your passion, take meaningful actions, develop **self -esteem**, create powerful habits, **master your beliefs**, and **build a better life.**

Happiness is the ultimate destination for the lives of nearly 8 billion people on this planet. Suppose you want to be a doctor, a pilot, an engineer, or a lawyer and became. Also, you earn a name and money. You have successfully reached your goal. What do you want now? Of course, you want **peaceful mind for a blissful life**, don't you? Therefore, all human beings have the ultimate and common goal of life: **happiness.**

Here is what you will learn in **PEACEFUL MIND FOR A BLISSFUL LIFE:**

1.   How to be **happy** -9 ways to find more **blissful in life**. Focus on relationship, don't look to money for **happiness**, move to a **happy** place and seek meaning in your life.

2.   **Happiness hacks for a blissful life.**

3.   Meditation for **happiness.**

4.   How to practice **meditation** for gratitude abundance.

5. Meditation for stress and **stress** management.

6. Recover from being cheated on by someone you love.

7. How to get rid of self-care hacks to find **inner peace**.

8. How to change your beliefs by making positive affirmations part of your life.

9. 7 ways to program your subconscious mind.

10. How does your **mind and body** get **peace and happiness?**

11. How to keep your brain healthy and happy.

12. How to get **happiness** and success through intrinsic motivation.

13. What is the reason why rich people are **unhappy?**

14. Why is **mindfulness** popular in the world and the benefits?

15. How to control our mind from inner
and outer world.

16. What are the ways to control your anger management?

17. The secrets of 2 inseparable sides of **Blissful life**.

Do you want to experience peaceful mind and happiness all the time, take your first step to live in **PEACEFUL MIND FOR A BLISSFUL LIFE** and transform your life. Please scroll up and click the BUY button now.